A LOOK AT LIFE CYCLES

Bird Life Cycles

I0869256

BY BRAY JACOBSON

Gareth Stevens PUBLISHING

CRASHCOURSE

Please visit our website, www.garethstevens.com. For a free color catalog of all our high-quality books, call toll free 1-800-542-2595 or fax 1-877-542-2596.

Cataloging-in-Publication Data
Names: Jacobson, Bray.
Title: Bird life cycles / Bray Jacobson.
Description: New York : Gareth Stevens Publishing, 2018. | Series: A look at life cycles | Includes index.
Identifiers: ISBN 9781538210369 (pbk.) | ISBN 9781538210383 (library bound) | ISBN 9781538210376 (6 pack)
Subjects: LCSH: Birds--Life cycles--Juvenile literature.
Classification: LCC QL676.2 J25 2018 | DDC 598.156--dc23

First Edition

Published in 2018 by
Gareth Stevens Publishing
111 East 14th Street, Suite 349
New York, NY 10003

Copyright © 2018 Gareth Stevens Publishing

Designer: Samantha DeMartin
Editor: Kristen Nelson

Photo credits: Series art Im stocker/Shutterstock.com; cover, pp. 1, 19 Butterfly Hunter/Shutterstock.com; p. 5 Ondrej Prosicky/Shutterstock.com; p. 7 (California condor) Kim Worrell/Shutterstock.com; p. 7 (rainbow lorikeet) jurra8/Shutterstock.com; p. 7 (hawk) Volodymyr Burdiak/Shutterstock.com; p. 7 (kingfisher) songwut tanoi/Shutterstock.com; p. 9 Julia Kuznetsova/Shutterstock.com; p. 11 percom/Shutterstock.com; p. 13 sysasya photography/Shutterstock.com; p. 15 (main) Tom Reichner/Shutterstock.com; p. 15 (inset) PJ photography/Shutterstock.com; p. 17 Master1305/Shutterstock.com; p. 21 Fsgreen/Shutterstock.com; p. 23 John L. Absher/Shutterstock.com; p. 25 Eric Isselee/Shutterstock.com; p. 27 adamico/Shutterstock.com; p. 29 Stefan Christmann/BIA/Minden Pictures/Getty Images; p. 30 Kotomiti Okuma/Shutterstock.com.

All rights reserved. No part of this book may be reproduced in any form without permission in writing from the publisher, except by a reviewer.

Printed in the United States of America

CPSIA compliance information: Batch #CW18GS: For further information contact Gareth Stevens, New York, New York at 1-800-542-2595.

Contents

Words in the glossary appear in **bold** type the first time they are used in the text.

Bird Talk

How do you know if an animal is a bird? All birds are vertebrates, or have backbones. They're warm-blooded, which means their body **temperature** stays about the same no matter the weather. But birds' most **unique** feature is their feathers!

Make the Grade

Even though they're warm-blooded, birds are closely **related** to reptiles, the animal group that includes snakes and lizards.

There are at least 10,000 species, or kinds, of birds found on Earth. While they live in many **habitats** and may look very different from one another, most birds follow the same basic steps in their **life cycle**.

Make the Grade

Within the general life cycle of birds, each species has its own special **behaviors** that make its life cycle unique.

California
condor

hawk

rainbow
lorikeet

kingfisher

Settling Down

Like all animals, birds spend a lot of time preparing for the next **generation** of birds. Before they have babies, birds have to choose a place where they'd like to make their nest. They also must choose a mate.

Make the Grade

Birds that **migrate** may do so to find a good place to have babies. They often claim territory as soon as they get to their chosen nesting place in the spring.

lovebirds

Mates are two animals that come together to make babies. Male birds try to **attract** female birds to be their mate by showing off, or displaying, brightly colored feathers. They may also bring the female birds food!

Make the Grade

Some kinds of male birds may do a little dance to draw in a female!

male
peacock

The Best Nest

Many kinds of birds build nests. Some use grass and mud. Some gather paper or other man-made matter. Nests may be built on tree branches, in bushes, or even on the ground.

Make the Grade

Each kind of bird has its own special type of nest. Eagles build big nests high on cliffs or mountains called aeries (EHR-eez).

Puffins, kingfishers, and bank swallows use burrow nests. They may make the burrow, or hole, themselves or use one they've found. For most birds, females build the nest, but some kinds of male birds help their mates.

Make the Grade

Woodpeckers are birds well known for using cavity nests. They use cavities, or spaces or holes, already in tree trunks or make their own!

burrow nest
cavity nest

Ready to Lay

All birds lay eggs. A group of eggs is called a clutch. The number of eggs in a clutch depends on the kind of bird! It also depends on the time of year, the weather, and how old the mother bird is.

Make the Grade

Some **tropical** birds only lay two or three eggs at a time. Wood ducks can lay as many as 15 eggs!

pheasant
eggs

Birds lay one egg at a time. Some mother birds don't start sitting on their eggs until they're all laid. Others begin **incubating** the first egg right away, which means baby birds in the same clutch may be born on different days!

Make the Grade

Some kinds of cuckoos lay their eggs in other birds' nests! These cuckoo mothers may even lay more than one egg in more than one nest!

The Strange Cuckoo Life Cycle

A mother cuckoo lays eggs in another bird's nest.

Cuckoo chicks are cared for by another mother bird.

Young cuckoos in cold areas follow their cuckoo parents and migrate.

Adult cuckoos choose mates.

Meet the Baby Birds

After a time, baby birds hatch, or come out of their egg. Many kinds of baby birds, including baby songbirds and seabirds, are born blind, featherless, and helpless. Called hatchlings, these baby birds need their parents to bring them food and keep them warm.

Make the Grade

Some birds, including ducks, have longer incubation times. This allows chicks to be more fully **developed** when they hatch.

robin hatchlings

As hatchlings grow, they're called nestlings. Bird parents are continuously bringing their babies food. They do this for as little as 2 weeks or as long as 10 weeks! Nestlings grow fast, sometimes doubling their weight a few times!

Make the Grade

Baby birds make a lot of noise, which can draw predators to the nest. Parent birds' continuous movement to and away from the nest can draw predators, too.

robin

Fly Away!

Baby birds grow flight feathers before they can fledge, or leave the nest for their first flight. Now a fledgling, the baby bird is still fed by its parents. After a few weeks, it learns to find food and fly, and it leaves its parents.

Make the Grade

Young birds have a very hard life. For almost all bird species, half die within the first year of life.

The Bird Life Cycle

Life of a Penguin

While penguin life cycles are much like other birds', they have some cool features unique to penguins. When choosing a mate, male penguins find pretty rocks to give females. Gentoo, chinstrap, and Adelie penguins all keep the same mate for many years.

Make the Grade

Some kinds of penguins make noise to draw a mate. They may coo, cackle, and even trumpet!

In almost all penguin species, both parents take part in incubation. However, for emperor penguins, incubation is entirely the male's job! The female emperor penguin lays the egg and then leaves until the egg is almost ready to hatch.

Make the Grade

Penguin parents take turns incubating their egg and heading to the ocean to eat. Female emperor penguins are gone for so long because they have to walk very far to the ocean!

Life Cycle of the Emperor Penguin

Glossary

attract: to draw nearer

behavior: the way an animal acts

develop: to grow and change

generation: a group of individuals born about the same time

habitat: the natural place where an animal or plant lives

incubate: to keep eggs warm so they can hatch

life cycle: the stages through which a living thing passes in its life

migrate: to move from one area to another for feeding or having babies

related: two animals connected by family

temperature: how hot or cold something is

tropical: having to do with the warm parts of Earth near the equator

unique: one of a kind

For More Information

Books

Christelow, Eileen. *Robins! How They Grow Up*. Boston, MA: Clarion Books, Houghton Mifflin Harcourt, 2016.

Kenney, Karen Latchana. *Birds*. Minneapolis, MN: Jump!, Inc., 2018.

Websites

Birds

kids.nationalgeographic.com/animals/hubs/birds/

Check out lots of different kinds of birds here!

Publisher's note to educators and parents: Our editors have carefully reviewed these websites to ensure that they are suitable for students. Many websites change frequently, however, and we cannot guarantee that a site's future contents will continue to meet our high standards of quality and educational value. Be advised that students should be closely supervised whenever they access the Internet.

Index